D1558795

FULCRUM

Selected Poems

Nirala Series

FULCRUM: SELECTED POEMS

The poetry of distinguished American poet and playwright Irene O'Garden has found its way to stage, e-screen, hardcover, literary magazines, anthologies and now, her first collection. Her critically acclaimed play *Women On Fire,* (Samuel French) played sold-out houses at Off-Broadway at the Cherry Lane Theatre and was nominated for a Lucille Lortel Award. O'Garden won a Pushcart Prize for her lyric essay *Glad To Be Human,* (Untreed Reads) Harper published her memoir *Fat Girl* (Untreed Reads, e-form) and her poems and essays have been featured in dozens of literary journals and anthologies. O'Garden founded *The Art Garden,* a performing literary magazine which she produced and hosted for twenty-five years. She now contributes to the spoken word event 650-Where Writers Read, in New York City and Sarah Lawrence College. Irene is also a Poetry Educator with the Hudson Highlands chapter of the national River Of Words program, connecting children to nature via poetry and art.

Praise for

Irene O' Garden's Work

For many years now, the poet, playwright, and memoirist Irene O'Garden has been a hero to me. I think of her as a walking, writing, beam of light. It is my hope that … numberless others will come to know her gifts and, most of all, her captivating talent for wonder and marvel.

—**Elizabeth Gilbert**, author of *Eat, Pray, Love*

Bewitching…astounding…heartbreaking

—**New York Times**

Lush imagery…poetry set to the life cycle of nature

—**Kirkus Reviews**

An immersion into what we relish, how we live, a kind of shining beacon that doesn't shy away from the tough stuff… Highly recommended.

—**Janet Pierson**, Producer SXSW Film Conference and Festival

Praise for

Irene O' Garden's *Fulcrum*

Fulcrum *is a stunning assessment of human life on the planet, a requiem of the mutant seasons when 'wind steals/ the juices from our eyes/our land cracks open / with an unrequited love 'and 'our mountains are on fire.'*

Experimental, theatrical and engaging, these poems are like molten lava of our minds, 'a single stinging tear,' a howl of every heart, a garland of 'offered images' on the altar of life, 'funeral of funerals themselves,' and a song of 'American shame (that) brings us to our knees.'

This is a newer version of The Waste Land, *a metaphoric pyramid of natural elements whose admirations 'blooms like*

fruit,' a casebook of the wounds of life and the wisdom you draw out of them. Like splinter of a stone that the poet once stepped on never came out, the poems once read will become part of you and help you 'know the knowing that we know.'

—**Yuyutsu Sharma**, Himalayan Poet, author of *Quaking Cantos; Nepal Earthquake Poems* and *A Blizzard in my Bones: New York Poems*

In a far-ranging and elegant suite of poems, Irene O'Garden balances a galaxy of incommensurates on the fulcrum of a disciplined intelligence. "I am a blueprint of a holy universe" seesaws against "I feel like a set of china"—the former in a Herbert-like sacred meditation, the latter in a narrative about being chased by a bull. Her technique suggests influences ranging from Donne to Bishop, from Frost to Moore. Soulful and rewarding, these poems remind us that "We're not made of matter but of mattering.

—**T.R. Hummer,** whose poems appear in *The New Yorker, Best of American Poetry, Harper's, Atlantic Monthly, Paris Review,* and twelve volumes of his own.

Having delighted in and been enlightened by Irene's eloquent human poetics for over two decades, I was kind of shocked when she told me this was her first published poetry collection. I couldn't quite believe it. Then I checked all her warmly gifted and gratefully shared titles on my bookshelf and yes, indeed, this was her first poetry collection.

And thus, Fulcrum, *where we all balance and* "blossom like a love-mussed bed." *Like* "a wound in the noon of a life." *Language hinging on voice. Voice on the cyclone currents of our aches and pains. Our joy and promise. The realization that* "I sing a thanking song." *And* "caress creation's verbs."

—**Mike Jurkovic**, curmudgeon poet, VP, Calling All Poets

Fulcrum

Selected Poems by

Irene O'Garden

Nirala

Nirala Publications
G.P.O. Box 7004
Munish Plaza, Ansari Road
Daryaganj, New Delhi-110002
niralabooks@yahoo.co.in
www.niralapublications.com

First Edition 2017

ISBN : 9-788182-500860

Cover Design by Shailendra Saxena

Author Photo: Mark Lacko

Where applicable quotes used with permission of the authors.

Printed at
Chaman Offset Press
New Delhi-2

Acknowledgments

Profound thanks to the journals and anthologies who first published the work inside this book. Their names are found on page 85. Anyone who reads or runs a literary magazine keeps us alive.

Poets and poetry thrive on friendship. For years of wonderful conversations and support, thank you to Jean Marzollo (who loves poetry almost more than anyone) and Patricia Adams. Thanks to Jorie Latham for close reading and good advice; Vay David, for quinces and other delicacies; Tracy Strong and Cecile Lindstedt, for showing up and listening. Hats off to Mark Lacko, who keeps mending my dictionary stand.

Robin O'Brien, your unflagging support and love are indispensable.

Thanks to my steadfast agent, Anne Marie O'Farrell; my ever-committed editor, Yuyutsu Sharma; Managing Director, Suresh Verma, Designer, Tanmay Sardar, Cover Designer, Shailendra Saxena and everyone at Nirala Publications. Particular thanks to my sensitive fellow poet Christi Shannon Kline. Without them, this book would not exist.

Thanks to these small but mighty organizations: The Garrison Art Center, The Philipstown Depot Theatre, and Calling All Poets who offer space and support for readings. Special gratitude to the Hudson Highlands Land Trust, for its ongoing commitment to the River of Words program which inspires young poets.

Contents

FULCRUM:

1. The point on which a lever is placed to get a purchase
or on which it turns
or is supported.

2. A thing that plays a central or essential role
in an activity, event, or situation.

—Oxford Dictionary of English

For John, who is my fulcrum, lover and lever.

FULCRUM
Selected Poems

AESTHETICS

Sublimely drawn in brick-red chalk on marble I saw once
an exquisite profile—the masterpiece an artist haunts
a lifetime for. Then truth tripped beauty in disdain.
A closer look: the splendor is a stain.
No pinnacle of art, no hand's creation—
just discolored stone. Porous imagination!
Images flow through like rain through rock,
which cause and yet offset the shock:
for that which uses mind, not hand, to draw
asks only that we see and say we saw.

NONFICTION

It is nonfiction, how I loved the little squares
shelved in boxes near the radiator, sizzling
with smelly mittens after recess. "Pick a toy
or picture book," our Teacher said. Nonfiction,
how I scooped and trickled them like Ali Baba,
glossy half-inch cardboard squares, hypnotic
orange. On each, a fat black letter, lower-case,
not penciled, but printed with the mighty punch
of type. Me and letters sharing recess. Free
of sentences. Words, even. My child-eye, a loupe,
studies the swiveling baby ***a***, the thumb
and bun of baby ***g***, the baby blacknosed ***r***.
It is nonfiction, loving shapely bright existence.
When consequence is not confined to sequence,
meaning spills from every box.

This very land my child: innocent fresh blue cheek
of sky. The tantrum brewing in her cloudy brow
cries out for mother's love, cries out for mine.

CANZONE di PRIMAVERA

Shaken throats of birdsong,
tear-pressed grass. You stop

believing you can't believe
it's spring. Sleeves of dotted

beetles warm limbs of lawn.
Wrens climax in the plumes.

Robin holds out a jacket
of stars. Haven't all songs

been sung? But for the best,
which you have been saving.

What bird reserves her best?

DROUGHT

This a mutant season.
Clouds caucus and adjourn.
The sky's autistic.
The sun   just   stares.

Our trees desert
their leaves. Roots shrink
from one another.

Wind steals
the juices from our eyes.
Our land cracks open
with an unrequited love.

Lightning strikes
like murder in a city.
Burning spreads
like outrage underground.

These are not mists
on ancient scrolls.
Our mountains
are on fire.

OASIS

I long myself away
from Cairo's sweaty streets; stinking breath
of diesel squeezing in the battered taxi window cracks,
grit and sand and smoke and donkey dung and fabled dust.
Lungs long for oxygen. None near the brown canal.
Rubbish heaps pawed by goats,
whose hooves disclose the stiffened carcass of a dog.

I long myself beyond
the stench and isn't it enough to reach
the ripple of the many-peopled fields? The green relief
of watered wheat, the pale tips ripening; the greygreen rice.
Ludicrous burdens on tiny brown donkeys,
shaggy with sugarcane.
The children gnaw sweet bamboo bats of it; and still

I long, along long
oblongs of alfalfa; people lopping
emerald camel lunch and donkey dinner. Can't believe
the green is not enough. Past silver fountains: date palms
rising on shadowy hummocks. All food.
Food produced far as the eye can reach—
back to the grey accumulate of centuries.

I long like a child,
my sight crushed on pillars and pharaohs of granite,
on ancient stiff profiles, blinking back greengrey Egyptian
dust.
I'm longing for color, for fragrance for grace. Mash of pink
answers my ravenous eye. Geraniums. Come and gone fast
as a sneeze.
Long enough to reveal
that here flowers are luxuries. Mouths must be fed.
Make an oasis of longing and you will be dead.

(Note: I call the words and phrases in superscript "fulcrums." They serve the teeter and the totter of lines in which they are found. Fulcrums are read twice, and these poems are best read aloud.)

FATHER'S DAY

Never isn't only for the dead.
To earth you laid your sonhood with your father
massive as the stones he split and set
precise as well-tied flies his living care

runs rail and beam throughout the house
he built to shelter you will never enter
it again with joyous carelessness here
beaming from your face he framed the faces
of you all. Only paper pictures
left. Only never isn't only.

Beefsteaks bent with fruit he will not taste
Christmas looming like a leaden sky
without the sun of his delight in gifts
he taught you how to make mistakes
not matter nothing matters. Never.

Living isn't only rocketing
desire in your thumby son, whose baseball
broke a window in the sanctuary of
his yearning eyes, however, never's only cure.

(Note: I call the words and phrases in superscript "fulcrums." They serve the teeter and the totter of lines in which they are found. Fulcrums are read twice, and these poems are best read aloud.)

GETTING ON WITH IT

Why doesn't she get on with it and die?
She's so unhappy weeping, puzzling
I pack to leave blood vessels pulling

from this wooden womb, my home
a dozen years this stone grown part of bone
break, nearly, moving from this house
and land, leave leg and hand cups fallen petals
of anemones and memories

they say are all beyond her now
meanings, just old newsprint wrapping up
my precious salts and peppers me, that voice
of hers she cannot use, its sting:
now say good-bye to everything.

OLD SHRUB ROSES

Call us old shrub roses in our middle age:
the concentration of our power does assuage
our pang that only once a year we flower.

Certainly the pert tea roses gratify—
Their lipstick reds and lacquered oranges, tight and high,
Bloom all summer long—but they exhaust the eye.

Their stiff and fussy pulchritude, imbued with fear,
(marred by spot and mildew, to their shame severe)
is absent of all scent—such beauty's charge is dear.

Not for bud and cutting were old roses bred.
Little, then, our leather foliage cannot shed,
and we blossom like a love-mussed bed.

After salt and wind and wait and freeze and heat
our tough and thorny bosoms open, soft and sweet.
our blooming is a loosened loom of woven mauve
and plum perfume.

Call us old shrub roses in our middle age:
we endure, we adhere, we have by now grown sage
and skilled. The attar of a year is now distilled
in every bloom, and not a drop is spilled.

PRIMAVERA IN AUTUNNO

Primavera: velvet-nippled peaches.
Sun-buffed oak-shoulders. Slim-

kneed lean green grasses: fragrant
fate. Silver etching childhood-scented

fields. Apple elbows dogwood nudging
juniper. Young magnolia graduates.

Yes, lullabying doves. Yes, autumn vision
losing her precision. Yet, impeccable. Impeccable.

Note: I call the words and phrases in [superscript] "fulcrums." They serve the teeter and the totter of lines in which they are found. Fulcrums are read twice, and these poems are best read aloud.)

SERGEANT ELEANOR IS LAID TO REST

3

Sergeant Eleanor is laid to rest
in fields of wild yolk-yellow mustard,
her small flock flanked
by servicemen in [uniform] in every motion.
Sergeant Eleanor adored the service:
giving and receiving [orders] of nuns, almost—
army women in the forties. Peacetime
disregarded this fine [soldier] on did Sergeant Eleanor.
Two husbands, and a third man—
all without [honor] Sergeant Eleanor, for lives
she gave and guarded: this daughter and this son.
Purple-heart her factory work, her combat
with doctors, bankers, teachers:
Sergeant Eleanor [made herself] goddam heard,
despite the flaying bayonets of loneliness.
Single motherhood: countless acts of valor
and a helluva lemon meringue.
Three shots shock like broken egg [shells] fly
from barrels, soldiers lay this soldier
in the [grave] salute. The pierce of Taps,
the folded flag delivered, crowd dispersed.
Sergeant Eleanor's son and daughter
open the car [at the crossroads of dust] shrieks
from a rust-ringed feathered throat:

Kildeer at the right front tire,
fatherless her dusty gravel nest,
and yet two speckled eggs warm with life.

Note: I call the words and phrases in superscript "fulcrums." They serve the teeter and the totter of lines in which they are found. Fulcrums are read twice, and these poems are best read aloud.)

RAILS OF ASPARAGUS

Rails of asparagus
rolling in olive oil
roast and encarmel
on fierce oven rails
crossing rails crossing
keyholes of garlic all
crisped in the pan for this
gold: sharing asparagus olive oil garlic
beloveds are here me now
they won't always be
mindful of this. Pass the salt.

NOVEMBER

Wander down, chill,
as earth turns her shoulder to the sun
wan yellow mottled tissue grey sky

Wander down, chill,
chalk grey trees, chill soil smell,
stalk spore puff pod broom brown grass

messy tufts and crossing branches
chaos of the trampled stalk—
jostled shadows of departing forms
tremor in the wind
buds like pepperberries spiral up a stem
silent on the nodding nutmeg branch
a steady living still grey owl
whose underwings are teal and fuschia

Wander down, chill, and tell your tale.

Chill whispers dryly,
death makes room for life to give
bodies are for life to live
each in its own time, each must pass
out of the ether and into the mass
out of the mass and into the light
birth death thought flight
balance order grow decay
day within day within day within day

TO THE PERSON WHO WASHES MY BODY AT DEATH

Fearless of odors and toes, oh most intimate stranger!
I thought of you once,
and the service of kindness you chose.

You could be bathing a rose-bodied baby
or cleaning a wound in the noon of a life,

but you cradle my sunk twilight flesh.
Ever-arising compassion! Mysterious sap in
humanity's stem! Gratitude offers itself again.

FULCRUM: MARRIAGE

HUSBANDRY

Admiration blossomed like a fruit tree when we met.
Over time, our branches intertwined.
We opened bark and grafted, hot and wet.

We dispensed sweet succulent esteem
for one another's fruits, but for awhile
confused our roots.

I tried to grow an apple just like yours,
but all I grew was oranges with cores.
You tried to grow an orange just like mine,
but only grew an apple with a rind.

That was then and this is now.
We have a stronger sense of our own boughs.
Though we support each other sure as stone,
we understand our flavors are our own.

MARGARITAS

we imbibe
sweet salt lime
and dizziness
on a mexican beach.

you go back to the room
for something,
i cut my toe on a shell
and wander off for bandaid

you return
to a me-less table
embarrassed by your
staggering wife,
the stagger equal parts
blood and tequila

dreadful your embarrassment,
fierce i held my right to drink,
and not to bleed. Both angry,
dinnerless, you be this way,
no it's my vacation, too,
you be this way!

hot tears on the black crashing beach,
black ocean showing us oblivion
this poisoned night
as shocking as a cockfight
to us both.

some injuries we never understand,
but we forgive; another time
a splinter of stone i stepped on never came out.
it is part of me now.

THE PEAR

If I insist this object is a pear,
then it is all a pear should never be:
lumpen, hard, disfigured by brown
patches. Yet as the utter harvest
of our tree this desiccated summer
when a match strikes fear, this fruit's
a wonder. Our little bartlett sapling
strained with only hand-poured rain.

Us apart; you, strained with work, aware
of meaning—always, sent it off to me.
Its twisted stem is nestled in its shoulder,
just as a bird will turn from cold or twilight
into sleep, tired from the flight
conveying your love all this way.

Dipped in the bronze of words
will I give you this pear.
Dipped in the bronze of words
will I keep it.

MOSAICS

"Go off," I said. "Go heal.
Don't tell me where you're going
or when you'll be back.
I'll see you when I see you."

This you loved. You left.
I spent my busy weeks alone,
wondered where in the world
you went, Germany maybe,

gone to your roots, I mused,
paging through my books. "Greece,"
you said when you returned,
radiant, telling of temples,

and cultural roots, a visit
to an island with my name,
and, oh, yes, mosaics.
"Mosaics!" I cried, and I ran

for my book. "I've been studying
them for the last couple days!"
A bookmark stuck where the finest
were. "My favorites," I showed you.

You drew a sharp breath
and your palm struck your chest.
"I was in this church two days ago."

When we forget the mortar
that holds the image so, we never
know the knowing that we know.

(Note: I call the words and phrases in ^{superscript} "fulcrums."
They serve the teeter and the totter of lines in which they are found.
Fulcrums are read twice, and these poems are best read aloud.)

HOUSE OF SECRETS

What does our house ^{hold} fast
to ^{dreams} it is another $^{\text{being altogether}}$
secretly outgrowing ^{secrets}
agreeing into ^{being} selves $^{\text{a moment}}$
then ^{change} in the house of ^{things} change
^{change} unthings us
back to boneless ^{being} secret we ^{forget}
^{being} of sound mind we forget
Are walls $^{\text{the secret of a house}}$
is boneless breathless dreamless ^{being}
secret we forget $^{\text{the secret}}$ of a house
the door

APOLOGIA

I wanted to write you,
yet am I lost
in the voices of roses.

I wanted my pen,
not the coaxing touch of peach,
the goatsbeard's palomino mane,
the sticky resins of fertility.

I wanted to write you
of things more important than spring,
but my words are webbed in petals,
scattered over the fields
like daisy and bedstraw,
caught in the purpletipped clover.

I cannot gather or release them.
I cannot write or speak them.
I am lost in the voices of roses.

TO MY HUSBAND AWAY ON BUSINESS

I sit in my red chair under the green lamp
in the yellow room, surrounded by our mingled lives.

Together we arranged the boxed and bottled things,
at least a hundred dishes, nearly twenty feet of music,
our books intershuffled like aces and hearts.
Your gloves and mine nestle in each other's palms.

You hear this squeaky drawer, the shower sound,
responding birds, our dog's impatient voice;
you, too, saw the sky through the rafters last fall
when the house was re-roofed.

Each June we are together drenched in honeysuckle.

This red chair shares your warmth,
and now your hands and voice heartbeat the yellow room.
Beloved, how good of you to come
to prove by this green light:
no time, nor space,
just love assuming shapes.

FULCRUM: SPIRIT

IO SURVIVES

a true story

Ossabaw.
Always wild, this island:
vines choking vines, snakes breaking into eggs, cranes
plucking up fiddler crabs.
This old wild island saw Indians killed by pirates killed by
planters killing slaves,
made the planters leave their plows, loose their cows.
Tame turned wild. Cotton wed weeds.
Quiet-breed cattle bred wild. Wild were their sons
and daughters. No fear in them now. Masters of this place,
but for a farm:
island of humans at island middle
apart from and part of
the island's riddle.

A wild black bull has nosed
at the milkcow's fence for a week.

I first met him Wednesday at the woodpile.
His rock-muscled black back
dripped from the storm.

He mouthed a beard of moss
and would not let me at my wood
until he had appraised me with a hot black eye.

He shifted hoof to hoof, and eye-to-eye
I knelt and gathered up my load
and backed away.

When he saw me Friday
twenty paces off, his head shot
up, he wheeled, then like a quarterback,

faked left and right and started after me.
I startled ran behind a tree.
He halted and he puffed.

Pink pounded out
between his legs. A moment.
Pink withdrawn, he snorted and departed.

A man that night at dinner said,
"Cow tried to mount me once.
Plenty scary."

Saturday I started out for water. The black bull
left the milkcow at the fence to chase
me back inside my shack.

He snuffled my door.
He rattled my rickety windowscreens.
I stood there with the scissors in my hand.

After he grew bored and left, I did not see him for
two days but Tuesday I went sketching
in the deep wood.

Rustle.
I look up.

A dead tree-length away
the black bull hovers, sniffing.

He eyes me.
I cap my pen.

He frisks and bucks.
I trembling rise.

He's coming at a clipping trot.
I stumble to a tree and shake.

He halts.
Sound stops.

I peer out.
The hoofs advance.

I duck back.
We circle the tree.

To him it's a dance.
We circle the tree.

To me it's a hunt.
We circle the tree.

We circle the tree.
We circle the tree.

We wait.

He wishes a chase.
I itch to bolt

But clutch the tree.
I can't outrun

a wild black bull.

Grow bored with me.
Grow bored with me.

A minute.
A pivot.

He's leaving.

I'm sighing.

I stroke the bark print
on my cheek.

A crash
in the brush beyond.

We freeze.

A black bull twice the black bull's size
pulls out of the palmettos like a big black truck.
His huge black head is like a motion picture camera
which he pans across the forest till it stops on me.

A nod. A snort. The small bull backs off.
I scram into a crescent of palms.
Black light burns in the giant's eye.
"Hey, sweetie pie."

Bright knobs bob in the black bulls' bellies.
They chew chaw. I can almost see them spit.
The giant licks his dripping snout.
"Come on, angel. Come on out."

Be calm. Be calm.
Drink a little watercolor water to relax.
The bottle slips and crashes and
the black necks jerk.

The small bull kicks and makes his move.
The big one shoulders him aside.
"You got no class, boy.
This is how it's done."

Like an ocean liner,

his two tons of confidence
approaches, crushes plants.
I feel like a set of china.

What did Io do?
She had no escape.

She had no education.
Use yours. You are hero here.

Hero.
Who?

Robin Hood.
No arrows.

Peter Pan.
Climb a tree.

I spot a two-trunked oak nearby,
the Y thigh-high.

Peter you've saved me.

Silently as Tiger Lily
I back up against it.
Strong from splitting wood
I swing up like Zorro.

I look for Zeus' eye.
I tell him I eat steaks.
I say I am a human.
I say I can outsmart him.
I am Brer Rabbit and Ulysses.

I gesture up the tree and see
there is no climbing higher.

Looking down, I see
I'm only three feet off the ground.

A butting head, an angry hoof
can shake me like a ripe peach off this tree.

I lose my inner equilibrium.
I grab the trunk.

Red dangles from the black bull's flanks.
He rumbles like a diesel.
My fear is perfume to him
he's coming to knock me down

he's trotting

faster

help

a silver leaf detaches from my tree.

Keep calm.
Name this.

Fear.
When they talk about it
now I'll know.

What happens in this picture?

Human faces charging bull.

How do you solve it
without any weapons?

Life of Homo Sapiens flashes by my eyes

matadors cowboys Bedouins monks anyone
whoever faced a bull until
the-soot-and-ochre likeness on the cave wall.
Shaman moves you without weapons.
How? What power?

Power is faith in truth in motion.
What do you believe in?

i shake i shake. i can't believe, i won't believe
and see belief be bulldozed down again,
There is no truth.

Truth is what no one told you,
yet you know.

what do i know i know i am afraid and
guessing at the truth is all i know

Diagonals of fear stop shooting.
I go solid, raise my hand.
The bull oncoming stops.

The silver leaf is landing on the ground.

I speak out through my palm:

Out of this wood, Brother Bulls.

If nature took a billion years to bring
me here to name my fear
then by that truth,
I say you will depart.

And if that's false, and science is another human myth,
then by the truth of making myth,
you will depart.

If even that is false,
then I believe the truth of faith itself.
Depart.

The black bulls' stare is dense.
Blink. Blink.

A toss of heads.
A shift of weight.

Lust dulled, pretending to be grazing,
adagio they roam away.
A silence like an ended symphony.

i am weak weak frail feeling
great shaking waves of relief
my breath i held an hour breathes
i sing a thanking song

to Peter Pan and Mutual of Omaha
Cowboy showdowns showing being brave,
to scientists, the bones of shamans
and to whoever, whatever,
in my brain or in my mind,
my imagination or my instinct to survive,
the inside or the outside force
that is the shaman's voice.
Whatever that is. That shaman's voice.

(Note: I call the words and phrases in superscript "fulcrums." They serve the teeter and the totter of lines in which they are found. Fulcrums are read twice, and these poems are best read aloud.)

GAME

the child
believes in blocks anything
not the game enough
to play is not the props
the game is not the
blocks the child believes in the child

THE HANDS OF MASTERS

Stars and squares and crosses ray the flesh,
ripple knuckles, furrow inborn whorls.
Such glyphs are shorthand for the cords and coils
of process. Cup and slap, reject, caress—

creation's verbs reverberate these surfaces
(more intimate than faces— free of masks)
torqued and tempered by their massive task:
composing the intangible in space.

The hands of masters are the culture's thumb
by which we grasp the fortune in our palms:
meaning, which exhilarates and calms,
and wisdom, which is lost wax found.

OFFERED IMAGES

Lake a lid of asphalt grey
One for the truth in hiding.
Birchbark split in twenty ways
One for the hard deciding
Rosehip bright as prick of blood.
One for the writhing wrench of birth.
Fronds of fen-sprung ferns unfurl.
One for the lusciousness of earth.

Fishrib-slim pink fireweed frames
One for the caring hands of wives
Fugue of fungus up a trunk
One for the burly working lives.

Lilac rays of aster stars
One for the tender eyelashed young
Ashfruit blaze in laddered leaves
One for the rage of songs unsung.

Lightning-butchered Norway spruce
One for the witnessing of pain.
Maple dipped in tangerine
One for the pleasures that remain

Veiny yellow elder waves
One for the falling into graves
Burst and sodden thistlepods
One for the changing of the gods
Simple swerving cattail arc.
One for the mercy that is art.
Berry crown atop a stalk.
One for wisdom's silent walk
At last the clustered eyeflower blooms:
One for the opening of wombs.

(Note: I call the words and phrases in $^{\textit{superscript}}$ *"fulcrums." They serve the teeter and the totter of lines in which they are found. Fulcrums are read twice, and these poems are best read aloud.)*

REQUIEM for LIFE IN ORDINARY TIME

a suite of five poems (with a nod to Elisabeth Kubler-Ross)

DENIAL

stop $^{\text{the voices}}$ of ^{suffering} is it

$^{\text{the voices of suffering}}$ we want

to ^{stop} hearing the voices

of discord ^{stop} we say stop

suffering stop sounding $^{\text{no!}}$

no, suffering must be ^{voiced}

suffering's healing. Howling

baby's aided by $^{\text{her howl}}$

her protest and her praise

of ^{life} giving ^{howls} of ^{loss}

the heart of every ^{howl}

of every heart: $^{\textit{have}\text{ becoming }\textit{had}}$

the heart of suffering.

ANGER

Throw ourselves on the coffin and rage.
No separation of church
and state your business is religion:
our malls: cathedrals, stores,
our church and state your business is
the United State of America.
How it happens—none of our
business ransacking our treasury,
eating worth like worms eat earth,
watching people burn through their savings
of fifty sixty seventy percent
on these neighborhood banks rolling
off cliffs notes on economics:
buy low sell high sell short
bet hope against health
take crap then sell it
frayed nerves of steal the capital
out of Capitalism: ism's all that's left.
Ism falls like a Berlin Wall.
Ism falls like a statue of Lenin.
Ism falls like a calving glacier.

BARGAINING

Please, forgive our unexamined greed,
weeping as the cherry [blossoms] brown
with summertime's anachronous [return]
our cherished seasons, please.
We never guessed they were the [wage] war
on our philosophies, but leave us Earth.
If you but return our watered loam,
we'll plow our [share] your mercy. We'll ignite
our deadly toys upon a pyre of wisdom,
interplay instead with living snow,
with spearmint ether.

DEPRESSION

Dying polar bear market.
Hopes collapse like bad prefabs.
Derricks of rage blast diesels of blame.
Lead-hung lungs. Eyes decoct in sockets.
Cremation as and of a way of life.
Funeral of independent living
back with parents, or with children.
Dependence, American shame,
brings us to our knees:
Funeral of funerals themselves.
Bodies piling up in morgues:
people can't afford to claim them.
Fossil pollen's found on Stone Age mounds.
Honoring our dead is universal.
Let this die, let this way die.
No more paying to be human.

ACCEPTANCE

We, a world of widows, breathe this ash.
We bow. We ring the bell. We say the psalm.
Every suffered death brings some relief.

We thought it was have. It is *how*.
Have becomes had. How becomes now.

No peace in ceasing voices, but
in harmony. No harmony in have,
but how. No harmony in then, but now.

Have becomes had:
heart of suffering.
Heart of peace,
now becomes how.

JACKSON HOLE, YEARS LATER

The valley wide,
my mother's ghost at her beckoning happiest.
Leaving behind her dark parlors,
caught on the upward thermal
of birdsong, here she first opened
to soaring, pinnacled on snowpure stone.

Ghosting, here too, is her aunt,
who brought her like a daughter here
at seventeen, this aunt a writer who, as a doctor's wife,
relinquished writing, settled for an interest in Society.

Here, only the society of evergreens and one another,
the fishing doctor uncle and his guides.
Campfire swollen with stories,
lace falling into the dirt.
Each senses the deep motherhood
from which she draws her
images of children—

The younger, alone with her soul
for the first time ever,
conceives of conceiving,
dreams of the children she'll bear.
I, among them feel her wishes pulsing
still within this valley.
Packhorsing through these cabins,
unaware she's flirting with the cowboys,
my mother opens to her soaring.

The older, alone with her life,
beyond its pivot,
receives the ravaged visage

etched in the mountain, her mirror,
dreams of the children
her body denied her. Space here enough to hold
her sorrow. Its magnitude is cradled in these firs,
and still it salts this greying bosom.

And here, beyond disturbance,
save the occasional cigar and smell of dung
these two easily forgotten women remember
how to be a body of the body of the earth.

am I the timber
am I the fallen log
am I the hawk and the tumbled shell
am I the snow field
the bones of the boulders
the blade and the blossom
the song in the cell

Within and without
the peaks pry us open—
to look is to journey
the brimming folds.
Each life is an arrowing flight
of intention and joy
is intention enough
we are told.

How to be a body
of the body of the earth:
alert as a spider,
sharp as a fox bark,
watching the habitted magpie
strut like a nun who's completed her task;
watching the washing sky,
filmy with forms from Blake,
bend to embrace the earth.

That which was frozen melts
in a gush from the canyons.
The many-voiced mystery

whispers again: sooner or later
the heart returns to worship

Having sworn never to worship again
having dismantled what is unworthy
having been bored to distraction by worship,
having denied any need to worship
while admitting the need to bathe and exercise
and shop and pay and scrub and fathom and
charter and transport—
Sooner or later the heart returns to worship.
Not for the sake of the God and the Goddess
who will not be sweetened with measly sacrifice.
Not for the sake of the netted straw hat
or the pancake breakfast or bingo-paid missionaries.
Not to please elders or neighbors or friends
or to hear hymns again
or to improve ourselves .
Nor for the fear of the soul speared
and crisped on the spit of eternity,
Or even the good that demands to be done,

Sooner or later, the heart returns to worship.
Worship is her native exercise,
as a body on the body of the earth.
Beneath the steeple, dome or evergreen,
she limbers up, she stretches, and she soars,
on the upward thermal of reverence itself.

Preceding and succeeding, mother and unmother
fill the valley wide.
Ghostly whispers mingle, hers and hers:
"We found this in the wilderness, without the words."

THE THIRD DAY

The First Day

Feast of Christ the King,
St. Thomas Church, Fifth Avenue, NYC.

For the Kingdom of God
is like a man telling stories.

A rapids in geometry:
the vaulted ceiling,
rushing to a waterfall of
seventy stone saints;
carved curved currents
split by palisades of cobalt glass,
pierceblue punched
to the deep of the looking eye;

whirled and pooled and eddied stone
lilting down to the flowerlit altar
its linen complexion serene
its heart of inlaid precious stone
the alpha and omega.

Splendor on earth to the glory of God.
The mille-piped organ announces
the start of the painting
the sculpture the music the drama
the story of the murdered man,
that little lamb,
the story of the tortured murdered man.

Beautiful people in beautiful clothing
rise in the varnished pews
at the start of the thundering hymn
the procession begins
in the dazzling dim.

Sharp slap of light
from the gold of the crucifix.
Glowy soft light

from redrobed choirboy cheeks:
junior heads nestled like
exquisite chocolates
in starched pleated ruffs,
the walking choir a long red ruler
marking boyhood to man.

Vigorous and pasty men are passing now
in red-trimmed gold brocade,
as if the Book of Kells could promenade.
One holds the jeweled Holy Book aloft;
the gems: a conversation of the light.

And this is perfection:
this splendor on earth to the glory of God.
The holy men the holy men
let's be with the holy men
and we'll all be holy.

What a great loving lap to climb into!
This bejeweled mother smells so good.
She shines her silver cups for me to drink from.

Facing the people in stone,
not the people alive,
the man in the goldest garment
greets our absent Father,
and asks us to apologize.

We say *hi,* and *sorry*
that we've been so bad.
Mercy to us, glory to you, Dad.

The angel boys sing it so perfectly sweet.

And like a Broadway number,
a dozen men in tails and white carnations
pass a dozen silver bowls among us,
bring a dozen thousand dollars to the altar.

Deacon, bearded and intense,
reads an ancient letter Paul
wrote to his friends:
"Be good, you baddies."
Alleluia, then we stand.

Today's holy story:
Pilate asks the Lamb
if he's the King.
"You said it," says the Lamb.

In the middle of the pretty sights
and sounds that people made,
the spickety vicar says we are incompetent and bad,
and only this Lamb's Death
will save the day.

Only His Kingship of
sorrowing love, and of vengeance, dejection,
of poverty, sacrifice
will make up for just how bad it is
that we were born.

Mother pours out poison
in her silver cups.

And by the end
we all have thorns pressed in our heads,
flogged with thoughts of selfishness,
we drink the vinegar of shame
and bear the sinner's ridicule
strung naked on a cross of guilt and hatred,
lanced by our unworthiness.

The rage, unspeakable at such a god for such a world,
we put down like any uprising,
by disciplined legions of habit:
self-respect and dignity
embalmed, entombed, and left for dead.

God's punishment could not be worse than ours to us.
For the Kingdom of God
is like a poke in the eye with a sharp stick
when filtered through old church glass.

The Second Day

The Winter Solstice

Cathedral of St. John the Divine, NYC.

But the Kingdom of God
doth reach beyond the mighty jeweled halls
and etched plates and woven silken threads
through the voices of the angels
as they echo in confusion
through the gleaming walls.

Six thousands gather
on the winter afternoon
in a gargantuan indoors
arching black above
and black ahead.
Five thousand sailing paper cranes
pause upon the soaring Christmas tree,
a migration of wishes.

Altars buttressing
the manypillared nave;
a church a hundred people high.

A stupendous clear quartz crystal cluster
picnic-table-sized
radiates within the breathing ribcage of cathedral.

Six thousands fall silent.
Blue light dims the drums,
blue bathes the grand piano
and the blue-soothed saxophones.
Darkness rises like a soft warm pool.

Hung above us glows the rose window,
a great moon of colored glass.
We think to be alert for this dream's start,

but the dark is comfortable
and the window such a sight—
a paused kaleidoscope, frozen firework,
circled fractured rainbow,
the very starlike sight seen
after a bonk on the head,
a flattened tunnel of candied light
into whose heart you peer
seeing back into time at the center
and yes, there it is,
your own
origin

just as the tiniest distantest tinkling of bell
and the faintest heartbeat of drum begin.

Slowly more audible
and distincter tinkling,
other limbs and organs become ears,
reflecting on the skill and
subtlety of such musicians
to tune so slowly up the volume
such control—

until you realize it is three men walking
with a drum a cowbell and a tambourine,
just walking at an even pace
towards you

and this cathedral's so gigantic
it takes ten minutes to walk
from one end to the other.

The spotlight draws them
and past you
awakened into silence now.

Watch red light in a long cone focus
on the saxman playing
a lone wolf call,
a sad-eyed dog of song,
a haunted hound of melody.
As sad a sound
as when you found
you caused a person pain
and didn't know it.
howl and wail
sobbing dogsong

and when remorse
is too excruciate to bear

the drums burst mightily and cleanse;
a sudden thunderstorm of joy:
glad energy erupts
expands a thousand dozen ribs
bolts of multicolored lightning
celebrate the consort on the stage.

Then virtuosi
intricate and blessed
as the vining pea.
Burst of music
shimmery scattered sequins
flung from the window of an imp
tumbling glass beads of music.

Deep notes roll
like heavy bolts of coatcloth;
the great intended thunder,
the tremendous wooden cartwheels
of a piece called Turning Point,
to feel quite then
a very change of earth—

vibration music,
felt before heard.

And six thousands of us asked to
howl our greeting to the changing earth
and *howl* we do, like glad young wolves,
like adolescent boys, like risen roosters,
thousands of us, happy to make
huge noises in huge churches
howling till our inner signals
brought it to a close.
Spilling down cathedral steps,
swollen with joy and fellowfeeling,
knowing wolves are innocent as lambs,
imperative as shepherds,

and that the Kingdom of God
doth reach beyond the mighty jeweled halls
and etched plates and woven silken threads,
through the voices of the angels
as the echo in confusion
through the gleaming walls.

The Third Day

The Harmonic Convergence
My Front Yard, Cold Spring, NY.

But the Kingdom of God
is like my most humble and infantile self
which I shuffled away to a cave
because I had no room,
which grows great in wisdom and harmony.

And the Kingdom of God
is the self I have beaten and hidden away:
the innocent feelings, the anger, the fear, the regret
the happy animation and the earthen feel of joy
and depth of sorrow and forgiveness, lying still
and on this morn awakening
for it is The Third Day.

And here, dismantling the cross,
we take Christ down
like some old scarecrow at the season's end,
and say that this odd-dangled body isn't Christ,
this old bag straw man was just to scare us for a while, but

Christ he is the Farmer

and feelings, parts of selves like souls today are rising
from the tomb, all innocent and pure
transformed and made of light.

For the Kingdom of God
is like the force of gravity
and it will get you in the end.
And when these voices all within us all begin to speak,
they speak as one and here is what they say:

I am the wonderful soil from which life springs.
I am foot and fountain, I am the great beginning and origin
and I am worth gold and precious rubies.

I am pure and brilliant light.
I am the promise.
I am good and thorough and pure
and I am the best and finest fabric and the soundest wood
and the holiest seed and the finest fruit
and the best beyond the best beyond the power of money to
buy.

I am the dearest love I am the flexible alphabet
I am the most exquisite paper on which to write
and the perfect tool
I am the widest channel and the subtlest channel
I am snow and sand and seamless sky
and the clearest marble to carve, and innocent child heart.
I am the holy bed from which arises joyful union and I am
the careful bee pollinating open blossoms.
I am surging hearts of animals.
I am myself and well begun
and from me every good thing derives.

I am a blueprint of a holy universe.
I am a sweet flexible design for joy.
I am splendid wheels of words superbly chosen,
unrolling, unreeling.
I am the clearest bell of laughter and I am as clean as tears.
Always I am reflecting and absorbing light
reflecting and absorbing love
I am music billowing out over prairies
open, swooping, roiling, and the movement of the clouds
is as the movement of the wheat and there I am.
I am true.

I am as right as rain.
I am arising in my own mind
as all the iniverse is arising and arising
join me it is The Third Day
and there is still a temple, but the temple is not still,
a temple is blowing in the wind and circulating upward
along the stone of architecture like a paper cup,
swirling in the street in the slightest
conversation of humans.

And the temple is the catch in your throat
as you hear the dulcimer and cello and the banjo and flute
as it follows and flows and leads you
and the temple is in motion always like the gushing fall
of water or of conversation
and always I am directing my flow and changing it
with new stones thrown down,
splitting the flow; rocks in the rapids.
And where is the temple?

In the swaying treetops and the motion of elevators,
in the yield of plastic to the will
and the great motion of paper.
It is alone
and with each other.
It is within and out.
And now it is this
and now it is that
and it cannot be contained forever for its virtue is so mighty
that it bursts
from the confines of stone and definition and regularity
and schedule and custom and structure

for no structure can contain it,
for then all structure would be greater than the temple
and this cannot be.

But it plays
and continues to play
and divide and declare itself
in the goldsapped weeds erupting through
the snowmelt flushing the broken statues, ivywrapped:
nothing, not even the dead, is still.

And doubt is a big rock cast into the channel,
but the rock will move and the water will move,
and the rock will wear and the water will bear it away.
And doubt is a shadow cast into the light
and let it be so,
for the light will move and the shadow will move.

And the temple is greater
even than the custom of the seasons
and it billows beyond ordinary day and night,
so if it should be seen that
winter comes in summer
and summer blows through winter,
it is only the temple assembling itself anew.

For we are those who have chosen to witness, to feel
the mighty strength of pure energy,
the bare bald movement, motion, spontaneity of life,
of stretching minds, of godness unfolding,
and know that what is stable is the power,
is the love is the outreach is the blessing
is the joy is the discovery is the recovery
is the chuting rollercoaster and coming out
alive is the experience
and we are not alone
and we are not alone and we are not alone
and we are together
and we are together and we are together

and there over the mountain
and the desert and the ocean and the trees
and the prairie and the snow and the rooftops
is rising The Third Day the sun the
moon the stars the clouds the rain the candles the crystals

of all human hearts from the horizon rising now.
For the Kingdom of God is within.
Amen. Alleluia.

Poems Previously Published

Aesthetics (California Poetry Quarterly)
Bitten (Summerset Review, Calling All Poets 2015 Anthology)
Canzone di Primavera (Barrow Street)
Drought (Mother Earth International Journal)
Husbandry (Skylark)
Jackson Hole, Years Later (Atlanta Review)
Land Assessment, (Waywayanda Review)
Margaritas (College English)
Nonfiction (Willow Review, Willow Review Award)
Offered Images (Calyx)
Quinces, (Bayou Magazine)
To My Husband Away On Business (Whiskey Island Review)
To The Person Who Washes My Body At Death (Writer's Forum)
The Third Day (Controlled Burn)
What You Will Believe, (In The Arms of Words, Anthology for Disaster Relief, Foothills Press; A Slant of Light, Hudson Valley Women's Poetry Anthology, Codhill Press)

Nirala Series

A Series of Contemporary Writing

All Vows
New & Selected Poems
David B. Austell
ISBN 9-788182-500822 pp.194 2016 Paper Demy

Fulcrum
Selected Poems
Irene O' Garden
ISBN 9-788182-500860 pp.88 2017 Paper Demy

Out from Calaboose
New Poems
Karen Corinne Herceg
ISBN 9-788182-500853 pp.91 2017 Paper Demy

The Tin Man
David B. Austell
ISBN 9-788182-500792 2017 pp.320 Hard Demy

A Blizzard in My Bones
New York Poems
Yuyutsu Sharma
ISBN 81-8250-070-2 2016 pp.134 Paper

Inside the Shell of the Tortoise
Poems written in India and Nepal
A Spanish English Edition
Veronica Aranda
Translated by ***Claudia Routon*** *with* ***Yuyutsu Sharma***
ISBN 9-788182-500686 2016 pp.56 Hard

Your Kiss is a River
Poems of Love, Food and Life
Carolyn Wells
ISBN 9-788182-500532 2016 pp.56 Hard

Poemas de los Himalayas
A Spanish/English edition
Yuyutsu Sharma
Translated by Veronica Aranda
ISBN 81-8250-070-2 2015 pp.134 Paper
Collaboration with **Juan de Mairena y de libros,** Cordoba, Spain

TEN: The New Indian Poets
Selected and Edited by
Jayanta Mahapatra & Yuyutsu Sharma
ISBN 9-788182-500341 2012 pp.134 Hard

Everest Failures
Twenty Five Short Poems
Yuyutsu Sharma
ISBN 9-788182-500464 2012 Hard pp.48

Prisoner of an ipad
Arun Budhathoki
ISBN 9-788182-500570 2014 Paper pp.64

Milarepa's Bones, Helambu
33 New Poems
Yuyutsu RD Sharma
ISBN 9-788182-500327 2012 Hard pp.64

Garuda
& Other Astral Poems
David B. Austell
ISBN 9-788182-500389 2012 Hard pp.72

Annapurna Poems
Poems New and Selected
Yuyutsu RD Sharma
ISBN 9-788182-500471 2014 Hard pp.150

Inside Out, Upside Down,
& Round and Round
Poems Selected & New
John J. Trause
ISBN 9-788182-500495 2012 Paper pp.83

Safa Tempo
Poems Selected and New
Bhuwan Thapaliya
ISBN 9-788182-500365 2011 Paper pp.50

All the way from Kathmandu
Selected Jazz Poems
John Clarke
ISBN 9-788182-500426 2012 Paper pp.82

No Child More Perfect
& Other Poems
Christi Shannon Kline
ISBN 9-788182-500396 2012 Paper pp.82

Things Missed in Exile
New Poems
E. Avi Frishman
ISBN 9-788182-500556 2012 Paper pp. 49

Journey Though India and Nepal
Poems/Pictures
Robert Scotto & Lu Wu
ISBN 9-788182-500457 2012 Hard pp.84

Incident on the Orient
Poems by
George Wallace
ISBN 9-788182-500440 2012 Paper pp. 76

Lizard Licking, Donegal *& Other Poems*
Diane Hamilton
ISBN 9-788182-500334 2011 Paper pp 82

The Price of Heaven
Travel Stories from India and Nepal
Evald Flisar
Translated from Slovene by the ***Author & Alan McConnell-Duff***
ISBN 9-788182-500556 2009 Paper pp.140